# HOW TO ATTRACT WOMEN

## THE RIGHT WAY

*The Only 7 Steps You Need to Master What Women Want, Attraction Techniques and How to Pick Up Today*

**Dean Mack**

# More by Dean Mack

Discover all books from the Social Skills Best Seller Series by Dean Mack at:

**bit.ly/dean.mack**

Book 1: *How to Flirt*

Book 2: *How to Start a Conversation*

Book 3: *How to Talk to People*

Book 4: *How to Ask Questions*

Book 5: *How to Be Funny*

Book 6: *How to Influence People*

Book 7: *How to Attract Men*

Book 8: *How to Attract Women*

Themed book bundles available at discounted prices:

**bit.ly/dean-mack**

will any legal responsibility or blame be held against the publisher for any reparation, damages, or monetary loss due to the information herein, either directly or indirectly.

Respective authors own all copyrights not held by the publisher.

The information herein is offered for informational purposes solely, and is universal as so. The presentation of the information is without contract or any type of guarantee assurance.

The trademarks that are used are without any consent, and the publication of the trademark is without permission or backing by the trademark owner. All trademarks and brands within this book are for clarifying purposes only and are the owned by the owners themselves, not affiliated with this document.

# Table of Contents

# Introduction

Congratulations on purchasing this book and thank you for doing so.

The following chapters will discuss how to figure out what women want. We know, it seems like the answer to the age-old question is far too complex to boil down into a 7-step book, but we've gone through ages of wisdom to bring you the nuts and bolts of it right here! While it may seem like women are from Venus and men are from Mars, that's absolutely not true: both sexes are, indeed, from planet earth. The whole thing might seem to be a bit daunting for you, particularly if you haven't had much luck on the "Dating Scene," as they call it, but we're here to give you the tools you need to be a success.

One of the first things you have to figure out if you want to rock a woman's world is what *you* want. While this book does indeed focus on what women would want out of a man, there also is an important component of self-discovery along the way. You can't be attractive to a woman without also being attractive to yourself. This is one of the big "secrets" of the game.

Knowing what you want will define how you go about getting it. While "dating" may seem like a singular end-goal of itself, it really isn't... that's like saying the end goal of all "sports" is the same when it's not. For instance, the end goal of hunting is to bag your preferred target, while the end goal of football is to gain yardage and touchdowns. Both are sports, and both should end with "victory," but what victory means and involves depend on a variety of factors... and the rules of the game you're playing. We can help you with those rules!

It's well-known that most women do not like so-called pickup artists, but we're here to help you get your game down without even making it seem like you're gaming. It's true! It's possible! It's all in your hands!

We want to help you be the best that you can be on the bar scene, online, or even flirting with that cute accountant (or CEO) at work. There are many different ways to woo a woman and many different environments to do so in, and we're here for you every step of the way. We can't wait to get started, and we're sure that you can't, either.

Whether you are looking for a one-night stand, a relationship, a trust, or even that special somebody to make your wife someday, the information in this book is designed to help you along. No matter how rich or poor or conventionally handsome (or not) you are, the information in this book will work for you. Give it a try - we're sure that you'll be amazed.

# Part I: Introduction to Attracting Women

## Chapter 1: Ask Yourself: What Do You Want Out of a Woman?

One of the first things to do when you are getting into the "dating game" is figuring out what you want from a woman. While this may seem to be a rather straightforward process, there are several different kinds of "relationships" out there for you to pursue. Let's go through the basic kinds so you can figure out where you are on the scale and start getting what you want.

**One night stands.** You're probably familiar with this one; basically, you're just looking for a woman to shack up with for a night of passion. Probably the most "traditional" version of this relationship is the story of meeting a hot (or not-so-hot) woman at the bar or nightclub and then taking it back to your (or her) place to spend the night doing the horizontal tango. In the morning, you wake up rather confused and have probably left your wallet at the bar and can't find your pants. If things went well you get a breakfast of eggs, and you try to remember exactly what her name was (Kellie? Katie?) and make awkward conversation over coffee and toast. You leave after (or she does) and you never hear from each other again.

This is the most traditional tale, but it's definitely not the only way to have a one-night stand. With the popularization of the internet, you can even arrange - gasp! - *planned* one-night stands. In fact, apps like Tinder and OkCupid are notorious for people looking for no-strings-attached hookups.

This sort of relationship has its ownchallenges because it can be rather notoriously difficult to *find* a woman who wants to have a one-night stand and the ones that do likely have many potential male suitors lined up already. But if this is the kind of relationship that you're looking for, it's important that you are *very clear* about its nature; otherwise, you could end up with a drama bomb on your hands.

**Friends with benefits.** This is probably the most-prone-to-disaster variety of relationship that you could have, but some people can pull it off with panache. Basically, this is when you remain friends with somebody, have sex, but *don't* call it a relationship. Essentially, a friendship with sex but no romance.

The benefits of the "FWB" are numerous: basically, you get a constant stream of (assumedly) safe sex with none of the drama or work of a girlfriend. However, the trouble with this setup is that if you are *friends*, this means that you are compatible and if you are *having sex* that means you are at least moderate sexually-attracted to each other...oftentimes, this leads to one or the other party falling hard for the other. (It's actually just as likely to be you as compared to her, however, so don't let stereotypes blind you to this and let you think that you are immune to the love bug.)

Of course, a positive end to the friends with benefits relationship is an *actual* relationship. This is by no means a bad thing but it's definitely still a failed friends with benefits.

Probably the more likely (and depressing) scenario is where one of you falls, the other one doesn't, and the first one ends up lovesick and depressed with the second one ends up irritated because the original struck-upon bargain isn't being upheld.

There *are* some ways that you can pull of a good friends with benefits, though...particularly if you have a long-distance relationship or a "time limit" where one person is going to be moving away. Friends with benefits can work well in this situation, and many women are very willing if you're a cool dude and they also want easy sex.

**The sex relationship.** This sounds pretty similar to a Friends with Benefits arrangement, but instead of being *friends*, you're... just having sex on an extended basis and that's it. If you're scratching your head and wondering how *this* could be arranged... it tends to be most common in the kink community.

Plenty of kinksters get involved with their local BDSM community and have ongoing sex relationships with others that solely revolve around sex. These can be easy to find and maintain if you are in the right communities.

**The girlfriend relationship.** This is the relationship that combines both sex and love and potential cohabitation. This is probably the most commonly-thought-of relationship when "relationship with a woman" comes to your mind. If the girlfriend relationship does well, it will typically progress onto marriage and potentially kids.

This sort of relationship can be notoriously hard to find, even though it seems like most heterosexual people on the planet want one of these. It's not easy to find somebody that's compatible for you, as men who have multiple dating website memberships can tell you. Women have similar issues with this.

**The wife relationship.** This is often considered the "holy grail" of relationships, but since attitudes have modernized to a certain extent regarding premarital sex and having kids out of wedlock over the past 50 years, it may be becoming less common or desired.

Typically, getting married involves at least a few years of being in a girlfriend relationship and involves a serious commitment of both money, energy, time, and a lifetime promise to be together. (Of course, this isn't exactly guaranteed, considering how common divorce is these days, but... that's the idea.)

**The long-distance relationship.** This probably isn't the relationship that most people go for, but it does sometimes happen to people anyway due to circumstance... perhaps one of you moves away, or perhaps you're trying to court a special foreign sweetie who's on the other side of an ocean. These relationships are notoriously hard to maintain, just because you're completely missing out on the physical component, though the mental and emotional ones are all present.

Generally speaking. Long distance relationships are doomed to fail most of the time unless there is an endgame in sight for it. A permanent long distance relationship is impossible to maintain except for the most dedicated and extraordinarily people.

**The status relationship.** Think "trophy wife" or "sugar daddy." Typically, this is an exchange of wealth (typically the man's) for beauty (typically the woman's). Most often this is also a relationship that has an age gap as well.

Surprisingly, these relationships are often very much sought after by both parties. Plenty of attractive young females are looking for somebody to spend money on them and spoil them, and plenty of older, established men are looking for somebody gorgeous and young to have on their hip (and, frankly, to have sex with).

While the above is probably the most common arrangement, there *can* be other kinds of status relationships as well. If you can find somebody interested, these aren't hard to set up... but... you typically do need a lot of money to get one of these.

There are more relationships than what we have listed here. These are mostly to get your brain juices going so that you can figure out the type of relationship that you are interested in having. Once you figure out what you actually *want*, you can figure out how to go about getting it.

**The mail-order relationship.** We figure that we should put this here because it actually is somewhat common *and* a bit similar to the long-distance relationship, though it's also got some differences. The "mail order" brides of modern times are pretty different from those in years past; that is, you can wipe out all images of a starving immigrant from your mind.

One of the most popular locations for "mail order" brides to come from is Russia, and this is because Russia is facing a serious demographic issue due to its war losses (from WWII; yes, the amount of men that were killed in Russia during that conflict is still affecting the demographics of today's Russia), and thus there are many more women than men.

But the women who are looking for a mail-order relationship from Russia tend to be highly educated and highly accomplished women. However, what they're looking for is a Western man who will treat her in a Western way; that is, egalitarian. Most of these women are not looking to be housewives, or at least, not in their entirety.

These often start out as LDR-like, but you'll eventually need to visit her and meet her parents, normally. Then you'll marry and bring her back to your home country to start your marriage if it all goes successfully.

While many of these relationships do end up failing (there's often not a lot of courtship that goes into them), a lot of them end up being smashing successes, so definitely don't write them off if you're tired of looking around your local market.

# Chapter 2: What Do You Have to Offer to a Woman?

Here's the hard part. When we're trying to attract women, most of us end up with our eyes on the prize so much that we forget what we're actually trying to do - make some sort of connection. Even if you're just looking for somebody to take home with you for the night, you have to think about *what you bring to the table.*

There are many things that you may have in your bag of tricks all ready to help you get the job done. Think about some of these attributes that we're listing and see which ones can benefit you the most in the kind of relationship that you want to pursue.

**Attractiveness.** We may as well get this one out of the way. Particularly if you are looking to have a one-night stand of some sort, your attractiveness is going to matter a lot.

Now, the nuts and bolts of the matter are that some of us are born with this trait (if you are, you're a lucky guy!), and others of us are just not particularly gifted in this department to start with. However, just because you aren't "naturally" handsome doesn't mean you can't do a lot to help up your game here.

First, working out is a sure way to make yourself more attractive. While there is a point where it gets overdone - most chicks don't really dig bodybuilders all that much - having a nice physique can matter a lot. If you spend some time in the gym, it can pay off in spades.

Another thing is to pay attention to is how you dress. Now, what's considered "good dress" depends largely on the kind of woman that you are attempting to attract. If you're attempting to attract a goth girl, you're going to need to look different as opposed to dating a corporate lawyer. But making sure that your clothes are clean and fit well never goes out of style.

Hygiene is also very important. Make sure that you always brush your teeth, keep your BO under control, and have well-kept hair (body, facial, and head).

**Wealth.** Also pretty well-known. Of course, not all ladies are "gold diggers," but there's no doubt that wealth can help.

Of course, you probably weren't born an heir. If you weren't and aren't on the track to making six figures a year, you can make up with this by having a good sense of money. Live within your means. While being good with money probably isn't as much of an aphrodisiac as *having* lots of money, it's a pretty good second place and can take you far. Nothing is less attractive than a man in tons of debt.

**Education.** Studies have shown that education is becoming more and more important to women these days when choosing a man - it's not good enough to just have money these days, for most. While this may seem like a small matter if you're just trying to score a one-night stand... the thing about education is that it permeates your entire being. Think about it - you can generally tell if somebody is educated or not by means of talking to them.

Being educated can seriously help your game, and help you with women across the board, whether you're looking for a one-night stand or a long-term relationship. The good news is that you don't have to have a Ph.D. to be considered educated... you just have to be learned in certain areas. There are plenty of ways to do this... go out and take some classes in mechanics, or simply pick up a book and read about Ancient Rome. Find something that you're passionate about and learn as much as you can. This will give you conversation fodder and major education points.

**Companionship.** Most people are looking for some sort of companionship…whether it's sexual, romantic, platonic, or some combination of those things. One of the things that you have to offer a woman is your companionship… and the kind of companionship that you offer is going to be different for each male. This doesn't necessarily mean that you have to fake being an overly-emotional romantic if you aren't… it means that you need to find a woman who isn't looking for that.

This can be rather a nebulous concept to wrap your head around, but think about how you are with your friends or family. Are you a jokester? Do you dominate the conversation? Or are you a quieter sort of man?

You need to find a woman who is looking for your sort of companionship. There's a woman out there for every brand of man… for instance, if you happen to be the quieter type, you may do well with a woman who fills the silence *or* a woman who loves the silence. It depends on what you're looking for, and what *she's* looking for as well.

**Compassion.** If a woman is going to trust you enough either to take you home or to consider a long-term thing with you, she needs to know that you are capable of loving. We hate to be overly basic, but unless the woman you're after has severe psychological issues… she's going to want a "good man."

This doesn't mean you have to be over the top and turn into a Romeo that you aren't. It simply means that your woman needs to be somewhat in tune with your so-called "weaker" side. If you're all muscle and brawn all the time, that's going to be a turnoff to most women... they're looking for somebody who knows how to love. That is to say: don't feel compelled to play the part of a macho superhuman wall. Most chicks are not going to dig it.

**Security**. This sort of ties in with "wealth," but women want to feel secure in your presence. The *kind* ofsecure is going to depend on the woman. Some women want to feel as though they are *physically* secure with their man (i.e., you make her feel physically safe), while others are just looking for more of a "mental" variety of safe. If a woman doesn't feel safe around you, then she's not going to be interested in either sex or love.

And monetary security doesn't hurt either.

**Fun.** Hey, never underestimate the importance of fun, because fun is *very important* in a relationship. You need to be able to provide your woman with the kind of fun she needs to keep coming back. Now, the definition of "fun" will vary from person to person and also depend on their mood, but there are tons of ways to ensure that your relationship remains fresh. Some women will like outdoors excursions; others will want to travel to exotic lands. Others may be homebodies and will just love curling up with you and a movie to spend the evening with. But no matter what they love, they're going to want to share it with you.

**Sex.** Also, this, for the majority of heterosexual women who don't also happen to be asexual. If you're not confident in this area, there are plenty of help books that you can look at to give your performance the boost it needs. It's also important to find somebody who is compatible with you; whether you prefer whips and chains or if your taste is purely vanilla, there is a woman out there for you. Whether you want to keep your sex "traditional" or experiment with anal (both ways!) or whatever you want to do, you need to ensure that your target is along for the ride. This applies whether it is a one night stand or a long-term relationship. Sex is vitally important, and your woman is going to want it out of you!

Of course, the frequency of sex and all of that needs to be agreed upon as well. While it's generally "assumed" that women have lower libidos than men, this isn't always true. It's very possible you'll find a woman with a bigger libido than you have! The most important thing is balance; a bad sex life can ruin a relationship, so make sure to never falter in your attention to this major detail. If she ain't happy, ain't nobody gonna be happy!

Hopefully, this outline has given you a better idea as to what you can potentially offer a woman. We hope that you have found some of yourself in these paragraphs… if not, these are attainable by everybody by making a few minor adjustments. Become the man that you want to be before you attain the woman that you want.

Read on to find out more about the seven steps to seduce the woman of your dreams!

# **Part II: The Seven Sacred Steps**

# Chapter 3: Step 1: Meet a Woman

Of course, the first thing you need to do to start any relationship with a woman is to... meet one. This can seem a bit daunting, and, in fact, many men get stuck at "Step 1" for years and years. The good news is that your only option isn't the nightclub! That being said...

**Venue 1: Nightclub/bar.** This is probably the most traditional place to "meet a woman," or, as is often said across the pond, "go on the pull." Generally speaking, if you're looking out at the club or the late night bar for a lady, you're looking for a one-night stand. While bars do enjoy a lot of patronages, the reality is that very few long-term relationships have started at nightclubs and bars. And, in fact, picking up women at these places for sex can even be more difficult than it seems like it should be.

Again, we go back to the "security" issue. A woman is going to have to feel secure enough for you to go home with you, and it can be difficult to communicate that you are not actually an ax murderer while the bass is being dropped on the floor. Again, these places can help you get lucky, but you'll do much better at them if you score high on wealth and attractiveness.

**Venue 2: Happy Hour.** This is like picking somebody up at the bar, but the more sophisticated version of it. Happy Hour is at a far earlier point in the day, so women aren't automatically going to assume the only thing you're out for is a quick lay (so if you are, you should be clear about this to a certain extent). Happy Hours attract people because of their great drink prices, and many will also have wonderful Happy Hour menus, as well. You can certainly get across your money-savvy-nature here, *and* pick up quite a few drinks that won't wreck your wallet. Combine with some apps, and you're off to having a great conversation with that cutie on the other side of the bar giving you side-eye.

**Venue 3: Intramural Sports Teams.** No, we're not saying that you have to sign up for a triathlon (but if you want to, go for it!), but joining a local team centered around an "indie" sport like dodgeball, ultimate frisbee, softball, etc., is a great way to get out there and meet women. The entire point of these teams is essentially to meet new people and then go to the bar afterward anyway. This is a wonderful way to pick up women and get across your "companionship" and "security" vibes. Plus, a lady who's playing sports is more likely to be a fit lady, so that's a plus!

**Venue 4: Concerts.** The good thing about meeting a lady at a concert is that you have automatic conversation fodder: you likely already like the same band. This is a wonderful way to connect with a stranger without giving off "creepy" vibes. If it's a concert where you can dance, *leave the grinding at home*. Particularly if you can smile and make jokes a bit on the dance floor, most women will find this enjoyable. Ask her about her favorite songs, other bands that she recommends... and so on. Easy, not creepy, fun.

**Venue 5: Dog park.** Do not attempt if you don't have a dog. Then it's just going to come across as stalkery. But if you *do* happen to have a dog, the dog park is a great place to connect over Fido playing with Sparky. Perhaps you could arrange a playdate between your pup and the one of that cute-looking brunette over there? (Of course, you're going to need to ensure that your dogs can actually play safely together...otherwise, you risk sounding like you want to hurt your target's Chihuahua if you're walking a Doberman.)

**Venue 6: Athletic events.** Particularly at baseball games, and particularly in the bleacher seats. (Most people there aren't paying *too* much attention to the game, anyway; they're just drinking and chatting.) If you find a lovely lady dressed in your colors, strike up a conversation. Baseball games generally last for hours, so you've got plenty of time to get to know each other.

**Venue 7: Pub Quiz Night.** No matter where you live, you'll be able to find a bar/pub that has a quiz night. This is a *great* way to meet women who are sociable and smart. This is a bang-on place to display that "education" tool and appear educated and fun. There's nothing better than celebrating a great win at trivia! And even if you don't win... hey. You've got a conversation starter.

**Venue 8: Church/other place of worship.** Obviously, this is restricted to those of you that actually have areligious belief - unless you want to cruise over to the American Atheists meeting. Since it is a house of worship, you probably don't want to attempt picking up chicks for one-night stands here, but it *is* a good place to meet potentially single women who may be looking to settle down, depending on your age and the norms of that particular religion. In fact, if you show up as an eligible bachelor, some of the elderly grandmothers may be willing to help you set up a match!

**Venue 9: Through work.** This one is actually much more common than most people would like to admit, probably because it has the potential to get you into hot water. If you want to try and flirt with that cutie in the next cubicle, you may want to read up on conduct expectations for employees in your company. You may be unable to fraternize due to company rules, particularly if one of you is in a subordinate position. Though, again, people romancing behind closed office doors isn't a common porn theme for no reason; it happens all the time. If you want to proceed, be *careful* and understand the rules. You *will* have plenty of things to talk about, from the latest project to management's latest snafu.

**Venue 10: Through the internet.** Well, this is de rigeur these days, basically. People tend to meet up through the internet more and more often... and the good news is that people who are on online dating sites are unlikely to be creeped out by you right away, as it's a dating site. However, actually getting attention from a woman on a dating site can seem like standing in a crowd and trying to get the attention of Mick Jagger on stage.

You can up your chances by having a well-written profile with flattering profile pics, and by using sites like Bumble, where women actually have to contact the men. Less wasted time on your part!

# Chapter 4: Be Attractive to Women

Easier said than done, right? If only we could all wave a magic wand and go "poof… now I'm attractive!" Unfortunately, it's not all that easy to do, but we can provide some tips to cover all your bases.

**Get a gym membership.** Face it: women like fit men. You don't necessarily have to be jacked, but being in good shape is going to go *a long way* toward attracting your dream girl, particularly if your dream girl is a 10/10 on the looks scale. Those women have a lot of competition going for them, and they know it, and they're not going to settle for substandard physical goods (why should they?). Even if you're not going after the hottest woman on the block, it's going to help if you're at least tone and spry. No matter how old you are, it's never too late to go to the gym.

**Concentrate on career advancement.** In many ways, it's been noted that the roles change considerably between men and women as they age. When everybody is younger, it may seem as though women hold all the cards, particularly the beautiful ones, since all the men chase after them. However, it seems in the mid-twenties there is a bit of a switch... suddenly women seem to be more attracted to the "decent sort that has a good job." Again, women are looking for stability, and one of the markers of a stable man is a good job that provides a regular salary.

Be career-oriented and try to become as stable in your profession as possible. If you do, you may find that a lot of women suddenly start to show interest.

**Own a pet.** Really, only do this if you actually are interested in owning a pet. If you're going to *neglect* the pet, this will a) backfire on you, and b) make you look like a horrible person. Owning a pet shows that you can keep something alive other than yourself (very good) and also shows that you're capable of loving something, which is a great way to show off your compassionate side. Additionally, lots of women do love animals and will love a man who enjoys them too.

**Be fastidious about your hygiene and appearance.** We feel bad about having to mention this one, but many men do need multiple reminders. If you have a beard, keep it trimmed, unless you're going for that lumberjack look. And if you *are*, great, but make sure to oil it and brush it and trim it regularly to keep it shaped and looking fine.

Own more than two "date shirts." Assuming you have more than two dates, she's going to figure it out and think that you only own two shirts. In fact, if you're beyond university age, it may be time to graduate away from jeans, t-shirts, and hoodies 24/7. Obviously, they're fine every now and again, but maybe try switching over to Dockers? Or at least button-downs with jeans rather than the constant barrage of "ironic t-shirts?"

Make sure that you have a well-maintained hairstyle (or if you're going bald, rock it well) and *pay attention to your hands and eyebrows.* You don't have to go for the total manscaping, but the unibrow never looked good on anybody. Keep your nose hair trimmed to a manageable level, and consider wearing *a reasonable amount* of good cologne.

**On the flipside, remember that women don't tend to care too much about appearance overall, in the grand scheme of things.** If you're balding and a little pudgy, that doesn't mean that your dating dreams are wrecked. Did you know that the happiest marriages tended to be where the man was a bit less attractive than the female? Women tend to care less about overall sex appeal than men do, a great deal of the time. Particularly as you age, this is going to work in your favor. This is also part of the reason why the older-male-younger-female is more common than the younger-male-older-female trope (though the latter is becoming more and more popular these days)!

**Learn the art of good conversation.** "Good conversation" is the modern man's flirting. If you're not much of a conversationalist, you're in luck - it's actually easy. How? *Listen.*

Good conversationalists listen. And, frankly, if the woman in front of you is boring you stiff with her conversation about her fifth manicure, then that's not the woman for you, anyway. You need to find somebody that you find interesting. If you're not the most avid conversationalist in the world, simply get used to listening to people and help them keep the conversation going. Typically, people *do* love to talk about themselves, so this is a *great topic of conversation for just about anybody.*

Ask her what she does for a living. When she does, go, "Wow, that sounds like it's hard. Where did you learn to do that?" and go on from there. This is a great way for the woman to start talking about a subject that she's very familiar with (herself), and you can keep on nudging it along from there. Boom, you're a great conversationalist, and you haven't even really had much of a conversation!

Also, check to see if she's asking about *you* at all. You don't want to end up with a narcissist.

These things will help you become more attractive to women overall. Remember, it's not necessarily all about how good you look or how much money that you make. Those things will definitely help you - but, let's face it. You'd probably be more interested in a hot, rich woman as well, so this isn't exactly a double standard. Plus, there's going to be a lot more women out there looking for decent guys like you (or fun ones, in the event of a one-night stand), so don't sweat it too much.

Maximize what you have, and work with what you got.

# Chapter 5: Build a Connection

Building a connection with somebody may be one of the most nebulous arts there is. This can be *difficult* even between men - think about it, how many *really good* friends do you have? Probably not more than two or three - and it can seem to be a Herculean task with women. Fortunately, it *does* happen, and the first step to making it happen is understanding it.

An emotional connection is based largely on *sameness*. We spend a lot of time categorizing people on a basis on whether they are the *same* or whether they are *different*. For instance, for a man, the woman is the "other." You're already in separate categories. If you are a Canadian, all non-Canadians are "others." If you have a certain color of skin, all other skin colors are "others."

We do this subconsciously, and we do it all the time, sorting people and placing them into boxes. However, in the case of men and women... even if you are the same skin color and hold the same passport, you are not the same sex... therefore, you are "not the same."

Or are you? Just because two people are in two different sorted "boxes" doesn't mean that there can't be commonalities between you. Just because two people have different skin tones doesn't mean they can't be friends. Just because people are from different countries doesn't mean they can't be lovers.

What all of those people have done is find ways that are *the same*. They have superficial differences, but their *emotional connection* has allowed them to find the sameness that exists despite that.

When you are trying to build a relationship with a woman, you need to look at your *sameness*. How do you do this?

**Avoid making highly argumentative statements at the beginning.** We're not saying that a healthy debate isn't warranted or that you have to agree on *everything* (you won't, not with anybody), but you don't want to inadvertently make an offhand statement about how gardening is dumb and then figure out that your target is a botanist.

Now, certain value statements can actually be helpful if you believe, for instance, that you couldn't date somebody who didn't at least have the same general political affiliation as you (some people can, some people can't); if this is a deal-breaker for you it may be advantageous if you get this out of the way instantly. But you don't want to blow it all on a stupid comment about plants when you don't really care that much anyway.

**Work on building a consensus.** Ask her for her opinion. "I was thinking about going to get Chinese takeout. Do you like Chinese?" This is allowing her to give her opinion and take a bit of control; plus, you get to learn more about her. And *remember this information for later*. Then you can work on…

**Giving looping feedback.**If she doesn't like Lo Mein, then keep that in the back of your mind. The next time Chinese takeout comes up, pick up the menu and say, "Well, definitely not Lo Mein, but you do like Egg Fu Yung, right?"

This shows that you are *listening* to your target. You can do this within the course of a single conversation as well; it shows that you are *listening* and *remembering* things about her. This is very important when it comes to building trust and rapport.

With these tips, you should have a lot of help when it comes to starting an emotional connection with your woman, no matter if you just want her for a night or forever.

# Chapter 6: Hone Your Communication Skills

As we've been more or less harping on for this entire book… your success with women will highly depend on your ability to communicate well. It's been scientifically proven that women are more able and nuanced communicators than men are, which generally puts us at a bit of a disadvantage. However, despite this, there are a lot of things that men can do to improve their communication skills.

The thing is that a lot of men never even bother to try, which means that if you really work hard on upping your communication skills with women, you are giving yourself a chance that most men could never even dream of. Even if you're looking for a one-night-stand, a good set of communication skills will take you to the moon and back.

**Make time to talk.** This is more of a tip for those guys who are looking for long-term commitment out of their lady. When life gets busy with work and other duties (or perhaps even kids), it's easy to let daily communication go by the wayside. Block out at least a couple of hours each week so that you and your lady can get in a good chat. You don't necessarily want to force the conversation toward the topic of your relationship (this might alarm her), but you can certainly let the conversation organically grow this way.

Talking about your relationship with your lady will likely please her, and it will go a long way toward making the overall tone of your relationship much healthier. But if you can't manage this, even a couple of hours of talking about the weather together will go a long way toward strengthening your relationship. If you want to be *good* at communication, you have to *want* to communicate.

**Give her the time she needs to say what she has to say.** Active listening, as they call it, isn't much heralded among men. Many men are either quiet and detached *or* have the opposite issue and tend to like to take over the conversation entirely. If you want to communicate well with your lady, you have to *let the woman have her turn to speak.* Whether you are looking to nurture a long-term relationship or looking to take a lady home for the evening... no matter how witty or how good at holding an audience you may be, *you have to let her talk.*

And you have to listen. Many men have relatively large egos and like to get their say in, and also enjoy having good comebacks. In this case, they are more focused on *themselves* and *their last word* rather than listening to what their partners had to say. This is a terrible way to communicate and often ends very poorly. You can't just give her the time to speak... you have to *listen* to her words for it to do any good.

Once you have let her have her piece and actively listened to it, start off your part with, "So, I understand that you're feeling frustrated about the living room being too messy for you." Basically, rehash what she just said in other words. This will let her know that you were actually listening to her. Try it. It works wonders.

**Pay attention to her nonverbal communication.** I'm not talking about mumbo-jumbo involving what direction she's looking in when she speaks, but the real obvious stuff, like crossed arms, narrowed eyes, an open, pleased expression, or the dip and tone of her voice.

Most communication is nonverbal. You *need* to learn how to pay attention to it. Sure, most people have their quirks, but some things are basically universal. If somebody has a tight mouth and narrowed eyes, you know for certain that they're not happy, right?

So make sure that you are taking these cues in and paying good attention to them throughout the breadth of your conversation. Don't just listen to her words. Listen to her *body*.

**Let her know that you care about her.** Even for a one-night stand, this is important to get across; most people don't want to hop into bed with a jerk. If you are in a longer-term relationship, you can get this across with touch - maybe a hand on her shoulder, or even a kiss (so long as the conversation itself isn't heated). If you love the woman, a simple "I love you" can go a long way.

Obviously, if you're out on the pull, you probably don't want to lay it on too thickly.

Good communication takes a while to learn, but it is *so very important* if you want to improve and maintain your status and relationships with women. The more effort you put into it, the more that you will get out of it, we promise.

# Chapter 7: Hone Your Physical Contact Skills

We're assuming that you're interested in actually touching a woman (who isn't?), so we're here to help you with that as well. With our advice, we can help you get a woman who is in the mood to receive a little bit of touch (or sex) from you.

The thing about physical contact is that *it absolutely must be consensual.* Non-consensually touching a woman is a first-class ticket to Creepville. That being said, here are some tips and tricks to get the ball rolling.

**"You have an eyelash that fell."** This one's pretty classic, but, hey, it usually does work... squint at her face for a second, and then reach out with your hand slowly - but stop before you make contact with her face. "You have an eyelash that fell," tell her, and see how she reacts. If she pulls away and puts up her own hand, that's definitely a "no," so drop your hand and tell her that she got the eyelash off. If, on the other hand, she doesn't back away, feel free to reach forward and gently brush the upper part of her cheek.

This is usually a good indication that she's receptive to your touch in general. This doesn't give you the greenlight to go all the way, of course, but it generally is a good sign. Another, less-intrusive thing to try would be "you've got something in your hair." Same story.

**Try taking her hand.** This is a good tip for whether you're just meeting somebody for the first time or if you're in a relationship with her. Initiate taking her hand, particularly if you are going to "lead" her through a room that's got lots of people in it. Of course, she doesn't *need* you to do this, but it's a good way to initiate contact in a non-threatening way if you're just meeting her *or* a good way to keep the contact up with your current lady love. This shows that you have great affection for her, and also goes with the "security" feeling that a lot of women adore.

**If you're dancing, make some contact.** Unless you are at a grinding nightclub and she's all up on *you*, you should *absolutely not grind on a woman that you don't know*. Again. Creepville. However, doing something like putting a hand on her hip won't go amiss. Maybe running your hand down her arm or something like that. Move a little closer. If you're dancing with a woman who is clearly wanting to dance with you, typically they aren't going to mind a *little bit* of contact.

**Are her hands cold? Take them in yours and try to warm them up!** Hey, no reason not to be a helpful gentleman, right? If it's cold outside and she's shivering, try to take her hands in yours and give them a gentle rub to impart warmth. It's likely that she'll get cold before you will - hey, women tend to freeze up before men do - and you can use that to your advantage, here. Again, this can be used whether you are already in a long-term relationship or if you are not.

Basically, get up some nerve and give it a go! It's always good to make a little bit of hesitation first, just to make sure that you haven't read her correctly. Always give her the opportunity to avoid physical contact... otherwise, you're being a creepster. But a little bit of boldness can go a long way!

# Chapter 8: Don't Forget About What's Inside

If you really want to know women off their feet, you really have to understand what makes *you* tick. We've spoken to a lot of men who desperately want women in their lives, but don't have the confidence to make it happen.

This is definitely a serious problem. To get love and respect from somebody else, you have to have love and respect for yourself. If you don't, then you're wasting a lot of time. You can't expect a woman to complete you; that's not how this works. A woman should be a complement to your life, not a completion. Otherwise, you're putting way too much pressure on her.

One of the reasons why relationships and sex often fail for men is because they're looking for something in their lives that they deem are *missing*. But the thing that's going to fix that is not the addition of a woman. You need to have your own complete life before going out and trying to get the attention of women. This will either attract subpar women or those who are looking for somebody to control and belittle. Neither situation is good.

We call this part the "inner game." Your "outer game" involves your pickup lines and your smooth moves and your communication abilities and all of that. These are the things that you are purposefully projecting to attract a mate for the evening or for life. What you also need to make sure is in check is your *inner game*, because if your outer game is based on a rotting interior, you aren't going to get anywhere at all.

What are the components of an inner game? Well, let's find out.

**You need to have emotional support from sources that are not significant others.** By "significant other," we also mean people that you are having one-night stands with. You may have heard that men have a considerably higher rate of suicide than women do, but have you ever thought of why this is?

We believe that a part of it is the fact that many men have subpar emotional support systems. Sure, they have "buddies," but the buddies aren't the ones whose shoulders you cry on. But the problem is if they *aren't* then whose shoulder *is it*?

One of the more toxic effects that standard gender roles have on men is the lack of emotional support systems that they provide for the male half of the gender. Often, the only person that the male feels that he *can* be emotional around is his girlfriend'/wife. This works just fine *until* for whatever reason the relationship ends.

At this point, the woman has plenty of friends that offer shoulders to cry on... but what about the man? Is he supposed to get by with a few pats on the shoulder? This will end up in internalized grief and is no good in the long term.

We're not saying that you have to go have a hug fest with your poker buddies and cry it out. But if your *only sense of emotional validation* is coming from women that you are in relationships with or women you are having sex with, this is a serious problem that definitely needs to be fixed.

**Confidence is key.** You'll hear this repeated over and over again in anything that even attempts to call itself a self-help book, but... what does it really mean?

Confidence is that thing that comes from within and allows you to be a stalwart man. It's what allows you to take on challenges and firmly believe that you will come out the other end. It doesn't necessarily mean that you always believe that you will *win* - this is hubris, which is not attractive - it means that you are confident of you ultimately *prevailing*, which is something entirely different. You can lose but still prevail in the end. You know, "Losing the battle but winning the war." Even the best general in the world has lost battles sometimes. But losing occasionally does not negate eventual success.

This is what confidence is. The feeling that no matter what happens to you, you will be able to get through it and get to a better place.

Of course, if you aren't inherently confident, you may be wondering how you could change this. The answer is "fake it until you make it."

That's right! By *acting* confident you will eventually *get* more confident. It's like the magic they never told you that you could make. Here are some tips for becoming more confident:

- Dress nicely;
- Pay attention to hygiene;
- Have good posture;
- Make eye contact;
- Smile;

- Make strides in your professional career;
- Have robust hobbies and friends;
- Work out regularly;
- Eat well;
- Sleep well

Basically, if you just make an attempt to live a good life, you will find that you will naturally become more confident. And this will attract women!

**Have a strong sense of self-worth.** Many of us do not, and that's a shame. We are all unique humans with the ability to contribute much to the planet and society. If you don't feel this way about yourself, your inner game is going to be very weak.

Don't be afraid to ask for help. There's nothing wrong with therapy and if you believe you have inner demons (from the past or self-made) that are preventing you from being the man that you can be, then getting professional help for the matter is nothing to be ashamed of. On the contrary, it's taking control of your life and ensuring that your future is as bright as possible.

Find causes you believe in, and only keep friends around that keep you strong (they say that the measure of a man can be told by the measure of his company). You are worthy of success and love.


Believe it.

# Chapter 9: Project the Lifestyle Your Lady Loves

Again, you are going to need to put in a bit of thought to think about the kind of woman that you *want* to attract. This goes whether you are just looking for a one-night stand or whether you are looking for the love of a lifetime.

The thing is, like generally attracts like. Water seeks its own level. That sort of thing. So if you want to attract a corporate lawyer, you are going to need to have the kind of lifestyle that a corporate lawyer may be interested in having. Of course, you're not a *mind reader*; maybe some corporate lawyers would be interested in the "power couple" setup and others would be interested more in a setup where you were actually the one who stayed at home... but one thing's for sure, they are probably *not* going to be interested in a surf bum.

Again. If you want to get a professional lady, you have to put out the vibe of a professional. If you want to get an artist, you'll probably be better off if you aren't in the military. That sort of thing.

Again, you're not mind readers, and we aren't either. But here we'll give you some tips on how to get the woman of your dreams.

**The collected, accomplished professional.** If you like a lady in a suit, then you're going to need to do one of two things: 1) Do the power couple thing. Love them or hate them, the Clintons are a perfect example of this. Both of them are extremely accomplished individuals in their own right, and both would be more than enough power to suck the attention of an entire party. Many professional ladies are looking for their professional partners so that they can rule their particular area of interest with them. This works best if you are actually in the same field together like the Clintons are both politicians. For instance, maybe you both run in investment banking circles, or stock broking, or IT, or anything that you could think of.

The other potential thing that a suited lady might like is... somebody who is a little more laid back. Actually, think of this as a slight role-reversal for the traditional "male as breadwinner, woman stays home" trope. This doesn't mean that you have to be a house-husband (but, hey, some women wouldn't mind that and if it sounds appealing to you, have at it!), but it does mean that your ideal lady may like somebody who isn't as "alpha," to put it, and a bit more laidback and easy going. Somebody to relax her at the end of the day.

Either way, though, these women mean business and probably would appreciate a living situation that is well-furnished and clean. A power couple probably hires somebody to take care of all that for them, but in a pairing where the woman is a CEO of the company, and the Dad is home taking care of the kids, it's likely dad doing the bulk of the housework.

**A housewife.** Maybe you're a more traditional man. You would like to be the sole (or at least main) breadwinner, and you'd prefer a woman who stays at home, takes care of the house, and raises the children. Not a thing wrong with this, either.

If this is the woman that you are gunning for, *expect to pay for everything while dating.* While the suited lady probably will put all of that Starbucks on her platinum card, somebody who is looking for the role of the housewife is looking for *you* to do all the paying. This is old-fashioned courtship, all the way. You need to be the one to pick her up from her house, take her out, and take her back. She may be a bit more old-fashioned when it comes to premarital sex (though, not necessarily), and she's probably the type who is going to want you to ask her father before you ask her for her hand in marriage, if it gets that far.

Basically, you need to be financially stable and have a job in a good industry that looks like it's only on the way up if you want to have success with this kind of lady. In terms of what your house looks like... you actually get a bit off the hook on this one, given that if your house looks like a bachelor lives there, that's perfectly OK... provided that once you tie the knot (or move in together), you give control of the interior decorating over to her. (If you're honest with yourself, you probably know that this is for the best, anyway.)

**The intellectual.** Intellectuals are all over the place, and if you're the kind of man who finds a lady with a litany of knowledge to be intriguing... you're probably one yourself.

This is probably the most important thing to the majority of female intellectuals; you need to be able to hold a conversation with them. An intelligent one. You don't necessarily have to be in the same field as her (though this probably wouldn't hurt), but you're going to have to be game for long conversations about the European Debt Crisis.

If this sounds like hell to you, you're in luck - you've figured out that you probably shouldn't date the intellectual type. These ladies tend to love knowledge for its own sake, and they need men who sway the same way.

In terms of paying, most intellectual ladies are probably going to expect to split things with you 50/50. It's no problem if your place is a mess; their place probably is as well.

Basically, the kind of thing you're going to have to project to get an intellectual girl into you is pure brainpower. And you either have this, or you don't.

**The debutant.** This lady often gets confused with her cousin, the housewife. And while most debutant-type ladies usually don't work outside of the home in a conventional way... they will indeed be high-society and be interested in hobnobbing with others that are of the same ilk.

If you're wondering why on earth anybody would want to marry or date somebody who's the epitome of a coiffed social butterfly... it's because if you are a man with a high-level job, you need a wife who can complement you well and also handle herself with aplomb. She will manage your social life and know the name of all your associate's children, and never forget to send birthday cards and presents. She is the one that will manage your social calendar, and if you've ever lived this sort of life, you know how important this is. Her "job" is like executive assistant, except for she's also her wife, so this business is important to her for more than just a paycheck. It's her status, as well.

If you're looking for this kind of lady, you need to have the cash to pave the way. Again, debutants are usually well-educated and used to a higher-status lifestyle; you need to provide this for her. Unlike a housewife, she's not going to do the daily chores.

Basically, project money and success and you'll attract the debutant. You may be surprised at how useful they are.

**The free spirit.** The free spirit is one of the hardest to nail down because she comes in so many different varieties. There are the "hippie" free spirits, and there are also the ones that globetrot.

The main thing about a "free spirit" woman is that she *probably* won't be around for too long. So try not to get attached (which can be hard to do; these women are often intensely interesting and romantic creatures), but the *good* news is that these types of women are less likely to care about your money or your house or your clothes or anything like that. They are kind of like intellectuals in this way.

But instead of *knowledge,* what the free spirit craves is *freedom.* So if you want any kind of chance with her, you have to give off the impression that you are not going to take her freedom away. Unlike many women, free spirits are not necessarily looking for commitment and, in fact, many of them are not looking for that at all. In this case, probably the best you can hope for is "friends with benefits," and maybe she'll fall for you.

Free spirits are good for one-night stands because that's about as long as they're around for. Tread carefully with anything else. Of course, free spirits can indeed decide to settle down, but...*they* have to decide that on their ownterms, and there's generally little you can convince them either way.

**The adventurer.** Adventurers are somewhat like free spirits in nature, but they are the ones who are actively looking for somebody to adventure with. Many of them are outdoorswomen and love camping/hiking, and some are more shoes that are meantto the urban climate. Be that in Bangkok, Bangalore, Berlin, or Bogota.

These women are attracted to men who think the same way. So if you want to make these women's eyes light up when you talk to them, regale them with tales of your time spent in multiple continents or when you learned how to drive a rickshaw in India. Homebodies need not apply.

Adventurers tend to care less for money and objects, and more about time spent traveling. Your travel lore, if you have any here, will help you immensely. Many of them are xenophiles, so if you're from a different country than she is, this may be more of a plus than it would be with other kinds of women.

The biggest aphrodisiac for these ladies is going to be a passport that chock-full of stamps and stickers.

There are many more kinds of women in the world; far more than we could ever hope to cover in a simple eBook. However, the fact of the matter is that you need to be aware enough of your target to understand the kinds of things that she would find attractive. What do you like about this woman? And what do you think you can offer to make her attracted to you?

# Part III: Some Final Tips

# Chapter 10: Final Advice

Now that we've outlined the seven steps essential to mastering what women want, we want to leave you with some general tips that we think could help you out there in the field, whether you're looking for your forever love or your fling.

**Be ready to interact anywhere.** If you are single, don't restrict yourself to flirting with women only at bars. While your conversion rate with women at grocery stores or libraries will be much lower than in areas where women are *expecting* if not *hoping* to flirt, you can still be effective here. Again, the thing is not to be creepy, so a good way to flirt is to talk about something relevant. If she's got an item in her cart, ask her about it. If she's reading a particular book, ask her how she likes it. You never know where an opportunity might present itself.

If you lack confidence, try starting with a general small talk with other people. Once you get this down, it will be easy to start conversations with those who you find more attractive.

**Axe the stupid pickup lines.** We all know them. "Are you okay? I was just asking because you're clearly an angel and it must have hurt to fall from heaven." That sort of thing. All this is going to get you is a groan or an eye-roll. Also, don't start off a conversation with a woman by asking her sign. This is such an old trope it's basically pathetic at this point. Go with something original. Compliment her on her shoes. Anything but stupid, corny pickup lines.

**Try not to be afraid of rejection.** We know; this is easier said than done, but the reality of the situation is that if you are going to swing your bat, you're going to strike out sometimes. This is just life. If you're going to meet the woman of your dreams, though, you won't get her by crying in a corner and wishing for your dream goddess to appear. You *have* to get out there. Plus, in the general societal context, men are the ones still expected to do the approaching. Sure, this sucks, and yes, it's not entirely fair, but neither is anything else in life. Try not to be afraid of rejection, and try not to take it too personally.

Just because one woman isn't interested doesn't mean that another one won't be. Just keep trying until you find the one that's right for you.

**Fifteen minutes is really all you need.** Particularly if you are looking for a one-night stand, you really only need fifteen minutes of conversation to figure out if she's going to take the bait or not. If you're looking for a one-night stand, a number of things have to happen for this to occur; first, she has to actually be interested in you; second, she has to trust you enough to go home with you, and third, she can't be in a relationship with anybody else unless she's in an open relationship, non-monogamous, or just out looking to cheat. You should be able to figure out all of these things about a woman within the first fifteen minutes of talking to her if you get enough practice in. This is when you'll know when to cut your losses or not.

**Also, know when to cut your losses.** This applies whether you are looking at a one-night stand or looking for a long-term partner. If the woman doesn't make it through the fifteen-minute test for one-night stands, graciously end the conversation and see about starting another conversation elsewhere with a target that may be more interested in you.

In terms of a long-term relationship... plenty of people end up in unhappy relationships because they're just so used to being in that particular relationship and can't imagine life being any other way. This is not a wise thing to do and is only going to end in heartache and headache. No relationship is going to be peaches and cream all the time, but no relationship should be a constant burden, either. It's also not good for the kids for you to stay together if you and your spouse truly dislike each other and the spark of love is no longer there.

**Be clear about your intentions.** Whether you are looking for somebody to have a good time with or looking for somebody to start a family with, make sure that your intentions are at least reasonably clear. Of course, there are good and bad ways to go about this: you don't want to be like "I want to have sex" as your opening line at the bar. You also don't want to be like, "I want five kids and a picket fence" on the first date.

But you should be able to make it clear in a non-confrontational manner that you have specific intentions. "It seems like you're a fun person, and that's great because that's exactly what I need right now; something not serious" should be pretty clear as well as, "I'm really hoping that we can take this further; I'm looking for somebody for the long haul" should also be clear.

Just be clear. There's nothing worse than a man who plays games. Don't be that man. You're better than that.

**Make sure that you close the evening.** Whether you're on a serious date or just cruising for something interesting for the evening, make sure that you "close" the evening if you feel like it's time. If you're picking somebody up, this generally happens when you've had a couple of drinks, and it seems like she is on your level. If you are on a date, this is when you drop her off back at her house/at her car/at her public transportation.

If you're picking somebody up, suggest going somewhere more private. At this point, if she's game, she'll know what you're intending. If you're on a date, make sure that you're clear that you enjoyed the evening (assuming you did) and that you will be calling her tomorrow to set up the next date.

**Don't play games.** In terms of "setting up the next date," don't waste your time with phone tag. You have better things to do. If she gives you her number, text her the next day. If you enjoyed the date, call her the next day and try to set up another one. There's no sense in wasting your time waiting two and a half days or whatever the new "appropriate limit" is. If you're interested, show your interest. Prompt communication means that you are a reliable person. It doesn't mean that you're desperate.

**Compliments go a long way.** However, be creative with your compliments. For instance, if you're trying to land a lady that looks like she's an intellectual, you don't want to make your compliments all about her looks. That's likely not what she values the most about herself. We're not saying don't compliment the intellectual lady on her looks at all - hey, she might not get those kinds of compliments often - but don't put all your eggs in one basket. Compliment her brains. Plus, don't go with anything like "you're the most beautiful woman I've ever seen" unless you're literally talking with Kate Moss. If you lay it on too thick, it is obviously going to come off as fake.

We hope that these little tidbits of wisdom will take you far, whether you are looking for a one night stand or looking for a wife.

# Conclusion

Thanks for making it through to the end of this book, let's hope it was informative and able to provide you with all of the tools you need to achieve your goals whatever they may be.

The next step is to get out there and start talking to women. Whether you are looking to form your first relationship or looking to score your latest lady, we hope that this advice is timeless and will help you no matter what your goals are with the fairer sex. A lot of this advice will keep you in good shape no matter how long your romance life is - and we do hope you live long and prosper.

Don't forget to keep your "inner game" as sharp as your "outer game." Whether you are insanely successful with women or if you don't get that much attention as of yet, you are still a worthy human who deserves love and attention. We hope that this book was the catalyst you needed to get out there and show the world how wonderful you really are.

Remember what women (typically) want and put your own spin on it. Don't try too hard - nobody likes a total conformist.

You are your own unique person, and you will find your own unique match in this wide world. Or maybe you just prefer the attention and fun you get with occasional nights out on the town. No matter where you are in your love life or what your future evolutions are, we hope you found this book informative and timeless.

No matter what your goals are, we wish you success and lots of luck with women and life!